AF269454

CHINA

R.L. Van

Big Buddy Books
An Imprint of Abdo Publishing
abdobooks.com

abdobooks.com

Published by Abdo Publishing, a division of ABDO, PO Box 398166, Minneapolis, Minnesota 55439.
Copyright © 2023 by Abdo Consulting Group, Inc. International copyrights reserved in all countries. No part of this book may be reproduced in any form without written permission from the publisher. Big Buddy Books™ is a trademark and logo of Abdo Publishing.

Printed in the United States of America, North Mankato, Minnesota
102022
012023

Design: Emily O'Malley, Mighty Media, Inc.
Production: Mighty Media, Inc.
Editor: Jessica Rusick
Cover Photograph: aphotostory/Shutterstock Images
Interior Photographs: ansonmiao/iStockphoto, p. 6 (top); gkgraphics/iStockphoto, p. 27 (bottom); hironai/
    Shutterstock Images, p. 15; Luftikus/Shutterstock Images, p. 7; lukulo/iStockphoto, pp. 5 (compass), 7
    (compass); Mlenny/iStockphoto, p. 13; Nikada/iStockphoto, p. 19; powerofforever/iStockphoto, p. 27
    (top right); Pyty/Shutterstock Images, p. 5; R Scapinello/iStockphoto, p. 25; reklamlar/iStockphoto, p. 30
    (flag); richliy/iStockphoto, p. 9; SCM Jeans/iStockphoto, p. 27 (top left); SeanXu/iStockphoto, p. 26 (right);
    shunjian123/iStockphoto, p. 17; Stefan Tomic/iStockphoto, p. 6 (bottom); Todd Jackson/iStockphoto, p. 11;
    travellinglight/iStockphoto, p. 30 (currency); Wesley Fryer/Flickr, p. 29 (top left); Wikimedia Commons, pp. 23,
    29 (top right, bottom); XH4D/iStockphoto, p. 28 (top); yanjf/iStockphoto, p. 26 (left); Zhang mengyang/
    iStockphoto, p. 6 (middle); zhangjin_net/Shutterstock Images, p. 21; ZU_09/iStockphoto, p. 28 (bottom)
Design Elements: Mighty Media, Inc.
Country population and area figures taken from the CIA World Factbook

Library of Congress Control Number: 2022940518

Publisher's Cataloging-in-Publication Data
Names: Van, R.L., author.
Title: China / by R.L. Van
Description: Minneapolis, Minnesota : Abdo Publishing, 2023 | Series: Countries | Includes online resources
    and index.
Identifiers: ISBN 9781532199578 (lib. bdg.) | ISBN 9781098274771 (ebook)
Subjects: LCSH: China--Juvenile literature. | Asia--Juvenile literature. | China--History--Juvenile literature. |
    Geography--Juvenile literature.
Classification: DDC 951--dc23

CONTENTS

Passport to China 4

Important Cities 6

China in History 8

An Important Symbol 12

Across the Land 14

Earning a Living 16

Life in China 18

Famous Faces 20

A Great Country 24

Tour Book 26

Timeline 28

China Up Close 30

Glossary 31

Online Resources 31

Index 32

PASSPORT TO CHINA

China is a country in East Asia. It is the fourth-largest country in the world in size. It has the world's largest population. About 1.4 billion people live there.

WHERE IS CHINA?
N
W
E
S
Russia
Mongolia
North
Korea
South
Korea
Yellow
Sea
CHINA
East
China
Sea
Nepal
Bhutan
India
Myanmar
Laos
Vietnam
Pacific Ocean
South
China Sea

5

IMPORTANT CITIES

Shanghai is China's largest city. It is known for its tall buildings and strong economy.

Beijing is China's **capital** and second-largest city. It is known for its culture and famous old buildings.

Chongqing is China's third-largest city. It is more than 3,000 years old. It is a major industrial center and river port.

DID YOU KNOW?

Hong Kong and Macao are controlled by China. But they have their own currencies and legal systems.

CHINA IN HISTORY

China was one of the world's first **civilizations**. Its written history goes back more than 4,000 years! For more than 2,000 years, China was ruled by **dynasties**. The country was led by **emperors**. Over the years, other countries tried to take over China. But it remained strong.

Artwork of a Ming dynasty emperor. This dynasty ruled China from 1368 to 1644.

The last Chinese **emperor** gave up power in 1912. This began a period of change. For many years, **Nationalists** and **Communists** fought to control China. In 1949, the Chinese Communist Party took over.

Mao Zedong cofounded the Chinese Communist Party. Today, the party still rules China.

1921
2021

AN IMPORTANT SYMBOL

China's flag is red with five yellow stars. Red stands for **Communism**. China's government is run by the Chinese Communist Party. The National People's Congress makes laws. China's premier leads the State Council, which enforces laws. China's president is chief of state.

The Chinese flag's large star stands for the Chinese Communist Party. The small stars stand for the people.

ACROSS THE LAND

China has forests, deserts, plains, mountains, and **deltas**. Rivers such as the Yangtze flow through the country.

Giant pandas, tigers, and monkeys live in China. Bamboo, larch trees, and peonies grow there.

SAY IT

Yangtze
YAHNG-SEE

Giant pandas are
an endangered
species. Many
are bred and
raised in China.

DID YOU
KNOW?
The Yangtze River is the
third-longest river in the world.

EARNING A LIVING

Chinese people have many jobs. Some work in factories making goods. Others help China's visitors.

China's rivers provide **waterpower**. Iron ore and coal come from its mines. Farmers produce rice, corn, and wheat. Pigs, chicken, and fish are raised for food.

Chinese farmers grow rice in terraced fields.

LIFE IN CHINA

Foods in China differ by region. Meals often have rice or noodles with meat and vegetables. Tea is a favorite drink.

For fun, many Chinese people play games like table tennis or mah-jongg. **Tai chi** and basketball are also popular.

Mah-jongg is a game of tiles.
It usually has four players.

FAMOUS FACES

Yao Ming was born in Shanghai. He played basketball from a young age. In 2002, he joined the **National Basketball Association (NBA)**. He played for the Houston Rockets. He also played for China internationally. He joined the Basketball Hall of Fame in 2016.

In 2017, Yao Ming was voted chairman of the Chinese Basketball Association.

Li Na is a professional tennis player. She was born in Wuhan, Hubei, China. In 2011, she became the first player from Asia to win a Grand Slam singles title. She joined the International Tennis Hall of Fame in 2019.

Li Na won a
second Grand
Slam title in 2014.

A GREAT COUNTRY

China is known for its beautiful landscapes and busy cities. Its land and people help make the world a more beautiful, interesting place.

Southern China is known for its karst mountains. These formations are surrounded by gorges and caves.

TOUR BOOK

EXPLORE

Stroll through the five-acre (2 ha) Yuyuan Garden in Shanghai. It glows with colorful lanterns during Lunar New Year!

SWIM

Visit the Beijing National Aquatics Center, home to Asia's biggest indoor water park.

SEE

Spot giant pandas at the Chengdu Panda Base.

DISCOVER

Study terra-cotta warriors in Xi'an. They were buried with China's first **emperor** thousands of years ago.

PLAY

Visit the Mutianyu section of the Great Wall of China. You can ride a toboggan down from the top of the wall!

TIMELINE

221 BCE

The first **dynasty** and **emperor** began ruling China.

618–906 CE

The Tang dynasty ruled China. This time is considered a golden age of Chinese arts and culture.

130 BCE

Chinese traders began using the Silk Road to trade silk for gold and other goods in Europe.

1949

The Chinese **Communist** Party won control of the government.

2022

Beijing became the first city to host both the Summer and Winter Olympics.

1912

The last **emperor** gave up power, ending more than 2,000 years of **dynasty** rule in China.

2013

Xi Jinping became president.

CHINA
UP CLOSE

Official Name
Zhonghua Renmin Gongheguo (People's Republic of China)

Flag

Population
1,410,539,758 (2022 est.)
Most populated country

Total Area
3,705,407 square miles (9,596,960 sq km)
4th-largest country

Official Language
Mandarin

Capital
Beijing

Currency
Yuan

Form of Government
Communist state

National Anthem
"Yiyongjun Jinxingqu" ("March of the Volunteers")

GLOSSARY

capital—a city where government leaders meet.

civilization—a well-organized and advanced society.

Communism (KAHM-yuh-nih-zuhm)—a form of government in which ways of creating wealth, such as land, factories, and machines, are owned by the state. They are shared among the people as needed. Something related to Communism is Communist.

delta—a triangle-shaped piece of land at the mouth of a river. It is made from mud and sand.

dynasty (DEYE-nuh-stee)—a powerful group or family that rules for a long time.

emperor—the male ruler of an empire. A female ruler of an empire is called an empress.

National Basketball Association (NBA)—a North American professional basketball league.

Nationalist—a member of a group that believes his or her country is better and more important than all others.

tai chi—an old Chinese martial art of gentle movements that improves mental and physical health.

waterpower—energy created by water moving machines.

ONLINE RESOURCES

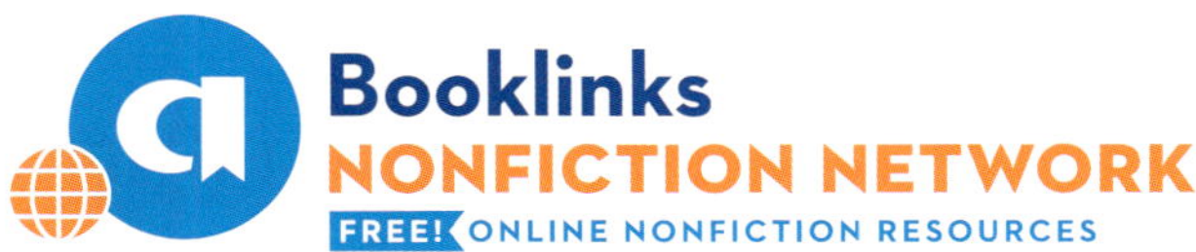

To learn more about China, please visit **abdobooklinks.com** or scan this QR code. These links are routinely monitored and updated to provide the most current information available.

INDEX

animals, 14, 15, 16, 27

Asia, 4, 22, 26

Beijing, 6, 7, 26, 29, 30

Chengdu Panda Base, 27

Chinese Communist Party, 10, 11, 12, 13, 29

Chongqing, 6, 7

dynasties, 8, 9, 28, 29

Europe, 28

flag, 12, 13, 30

food, 16, 17, 18

government, 8, 9, 10, 11, 12, 13, 29, 30

Great Wall of China, 27

Hong Kong, 7

language, 30

Li Na, 22, 23

Lunar New Year, 26

Macao, 7

Mao Zedong, 11

natural resources, 16, 17

plants, 14, 16, 17

population, 4, 7, 30

Shanghai, 6, 7, 20, 26

size, 4, 30

sports, 18, 20, 21, 22, 23, 29

terra-cotta warriors, 27

Xi Jinping, 29

Yangtze River, 14, 15

Yao Ming, 20, 21

Yuyuan Garden, 26